ON EARTH AS IT IS

ON EARTH AS IT IS IN HEAVEN

Temple Symbolism in the New Testament

Margaret Barker

T&T CLARK
EDINBURGH

T&T CLARK LTD
59 GEORGE STREET
EDINBURGH EH2 2LQ
SCOTLAND

First published 1995

ISBN 0 567 29278 9

British Library Cataloguing-in-Publication Data
A catalogue record for this book is available from the British Library

Typeset by Trinity Typesetting
Printed and bound in Great Britain by Page Bros, Norwich

For my children

Hugh and Katharine

Contents

Introduction

Temple theology is the original context of the New Testament insofar as the hopes, beliefs, symbols and rituals of the temple shaped the lives of those who came to be called Christians. Temple theology knew of incarnation and atonement, the sons of God and the life of the age to come, the day of judgement, justification, salvation, the renewed covenant and the kingdom of God. When temple theology is presented, even in barest outline, its striking relevance to the New Testament becomes clear.

There are no ancient texts to tell us directly what the temple cult was about, or to prove that its theology was the basis for the claims of the first Christians. Its influence has to be demonstrated by reconstructing what the beliefs and symbolism of the temple must have been. This can be done by drawing on the increasing number of non-biblical texts which are now available. Some were written in the early churches or were older texts which they used; fragments of others have been found among the Dead Sea Scrolls. Jewish texts written or compiled in the early Christian period are increasingly recognised as important evidence. This has become one of the fastest growing areas of biblical studies, especially in America. Translations are more readily available and serious students now have to study far more than just biblical texts.

For some people these 'other' texts present a problem; how do they relate to the more familiar books of the Bible and what is their status? In the Palestine of the early Christians, there was no such thing as a fixed 'Bible'. There were many sacred texts, some of which had already been recognised as having a special status. They existed as separate scrolls and not as a single volume. Some collections had already been formed, for example the scroll of the twelve minor prophets, but most were still distinct. It is unlikely that all communities possessed a copy of each of the books we now call the 'Old Testament'. Some would have used books we no longer have in our Bible, for example the Book of Enoch, which was used by the Qumran community and by the first Christians. Some would not have had access to all the books we now regard as canonical. Further, there were new books which had emerged in the Greek-speaking Jewish community in Egypt. These were not accepted as scripture by those who eventually defined the collection which we know as the Hebrew Bible. On the other hand, these Greek books became the Old Testament of the Christians and remained so until the Reformation when there was a formal separation of the Old Testament (Hebrew) from the Apocryphal (Greek) writings.

The discovery of the Dead Sea Scrolls has shown that even the text of the Hebrew Bible was not fixed. Several examples have been found which suggest that there were different versions of familiar Old Testament books; one theory is that there were variations in the different communities: one version in Babylon, one in Palestine and one in Egypt. Most of the differences are not significant, interesting only to specialist scholars; others, particularly where they affect 'Christian' understanding of the Old Testament, may prove to be very significant indeed. This is a task for the future.

Piece by piece the world of the temple is emerging from this mass of material just at the time when temple language is being *removed* from some modern translations the Bible. Thus 'firstfruits' (and all the theology that this implies) have been paraphrased out of the Good News Bible at Romans 11.16, 1 Corinthians 15.20 and Revelation 14.4. The 'mediator of a new covenant' in Hebrews 9.15 has become 'the one who arranges it'. This seems a high price to pay for simplicity. Students of the Bible who do not have access to the original languages literally do not know what they are missing!

Many of the new hymns written by charismatic and evangelical churches, however, are using temple imagery; they have rightly sensed that this lies at the heart of the New Testament message. New compositions such as 'Majesty' and 'The Servant King' now take their place alongside classics such as 'Immortal Invisible', 'Sun of my Soul' and 'Holy, Holy, Holy' as temple-based hymns. I have often used the words of 'Shine Jesus Shine', perhaps the most popular of all these new hymns, to introduce temple theology to a church study group.

In this book I have taken four aspects of temple theology and used them to show how details missing from the Old Testament descriptions can be recovered from other ancient texts. I hope this will both illuminate and enrich any reading of the New Testament.

Non-Biblical Books

The recovery and translation of the *Dead Sea Scrolls* since 1947 has revolutionised biblical studies. It will be many years before we know the full significance of this new material, especially for understanding Christian origins. The most accessible English translation is G. Vermes' *The Dead Sea Scrolls in English* Penguin Books, third edition, 1987.

Joseph bar Matthias, also known as *Flavius Josephus*, was born into a priestly family in AD 37. He fought as a leader of the resistance in Galilee after AD 66 but then changed sides and threw in his lot with the Romans. His works include a history of his people, *Antiquities of the Jews* and an account of the war against Rome, *The Jewish War*.

Philo was a Jewish philosopher who lived in Alexandria at the end of the first century AD. Much of his surviving work is an exposition of themes from the Pentateuch. It is the best evidence for Jewish thought outside Palestine in the New

Testament period and illuminates much in the Fourth Gospel and the Letter to the Hebrews.

The *Mishnah* is a law code in sixty-three sections ('tractates') covering all aspects of Jewish life. Although compiled in the late second century AD much of the material in it reflects established tradition and may be from a much earlier period. When later scholars explained the Mishnah their conclusions were recorded as the *Talmud*. Thirty-seven tractates were expounded by scholars in Babylon and these became the *Babylonian Talmud*; thirty-nine were expounded to become the *Palestinian Talmud*.

The *Targums* are Aramaic versions of the Hebrew Bible. The custom of translating the Bible originated in the time of Ezra (Neh. 8.1–8) when Hebrew was no longer the vernacular. There are Targums from the Babylonian and Palestinian communities, the latter often expanded with additional lore and legend which give a valuable insight into how the biblical texts were understood.

1 Enoch, also called the *Ethiopic Enoch*, is the oldest of the three known Enoch books. It could have been written in Hebrew or Aramaic. What is believed to be a complete text survives only in Ethiopic, but Aramaic fragments of four of its five sections have been identified among the Dead Sea Scrolls. There are also Greek and Latin fragments. The first and earliest section describes the fallen angels and the Day of Judgement. The book contains many old temple traditions and an alternative account of the history of Israel which condemns the second temple as impure.

2 Enoch, also called *The Secrets of Enoch*, is of unknown origin. It survives only in an Old Slavonic translation, but it may have been written in the Greek-speaking Jewish community of Alexandria. It is quoted in early Christian writings and so it must have been written by the end of the first century AD.

3 Enoch, also called *The Hebrew Enoch*, is attributed to Rabbi Ishmael, the Palestinian scholar who died in AD 132. It is impossible to date the present text as it is a compilation of earlier material describing mystical ascents to the heavenly chariot throne, the *merkabah*. Estimates vary from the third century AD to the fifteenth, but it is most likely that the final version was produced in Babylon in the fifth or sixth century.

The Ascension of Isaiah is a text of unknown origin, surviving complete in Ethiopic with fragments in Latin, Greek, Coptic and Old Slavonic. It is a valuable picture of Christian belief at the end of the first century, embedded in the story of Isaiah's martyrdom at the hands of the evil king Manasseh (2 Kgs. 21.1–18). The prophet ascends through the seven heavens and there learns the secrets of the incarnation. It is probably a Christian expansion of a Jewish original, but at this early date 'Christian' and 'Jewish' are often hard to distinguish.

The Apocalypse of Moses also called *The Assumption of Moses* is undateable. Opinions vary as to whether it was written during the time of the Maccabean revolt, at the beginning of the first century AD or in the middle of the second century AD, after the Bar Kokhba revolt. It was probably written in Hebrew, but only a single Latin translation survives. It is in effect a rewriting and exposition of Deuteronomy 31–4.

Chapter One

Reading the Meaning

All religious belief is expressed, transmitted and received in code. Even the simplest statements, when they are examined carefully by an outsider, have very little meaning. This is because every religious community has its own way of speaking about faith, and the most effective way to do this is in pictures. People brought up in a Christian community recognise immediately what is meant by the Lamb of God, or by bread and wine; to someone from another culture, however, these are not vivid images but a solid wall which separates those inside, those 'in the know', from everyone else. 'Other cultures' are no longer those who can be identified as other faith communities. The 'other cultures' now are the vast mass of people who have lost all touch with Christian tradition.

It used to be thought that putting the code into modern English would overcome the problem, and make everything clear to people who had no roots in a Christian community. This attempt has proved misguided, since so much of the code simply will not translate into modern English. It was not the words themselves which were the problem, but rather the pictures, the signs and symbols which the words were describing. The 'blood of the Lamb' is a phrase familiar to all Christians; it is perfectly good modern English, but, unexplained, is meaningless.

There has also been an attempt to put the Bible, more particularly the New Testament, into a code-free form. Remove the symbols and the pictures, it was thought, break the pure truth free from the story in which it was unfortunately embedded, and then all would be clear. The result proved to be exactly the opposite; a fog of contemporary philosophical jargon was offered in place of the vivid symbols and stories of the Bible, and the problem remained.

The task, then, has had to alter. The need now is not just for modern English, or modern thought forms, but for an explanation of the images and pictures in which the ideas of the Bible are expressed. These are specific to one culture, that of Israel and Judaism, and until they are fully understood in their original setting, little of what is done with the writings and ideas that came from that particular setting can be understood. Once we lose touch with the meaning of biblical imagery, we lose any way into the real meaning of the Bible. This has already begun to happen, and a diluted 'instant' Christianity has been offered as junk food for the mass market. The resultant malnutrition, even in churches, is all too obvious.

It is folly to approach the Bible with a twentieth-century mind, completely unaware of the codes in which it was written. Such a reading of scripture is not far removed from the reading of tea-leaves, and this does nothing to build up the faith of the churches. Rather, it leads to a trivialisation of the scriptures and then confusion.

Let us begin with words. Words which speak of God are never really what they seem. They cannot be taken literally. The Bible speaks of God as a shepherd (Is. 40.11), a father (Is. 63.16), a mother (Is. 42.14), a warrior (Is. 42.13). These are examples drawn at random from one book. In each case we have to insert the word 'like' as we read. God is 'like a warrior', 'like a mother', 'like a shepherd'. The images are drawn from everyday life. God has 'hands' (Is. 48.13) and 'feet' (Is. 66.1), 'eyes' (Is. 49.5) and 'ears' (Is. 59.1). He 'treads a wine press' (Is. 63.3) and 'forsakes his wife' (Is. 54.5–8). Again, the word 'like' has to be read into the words every time we see them, because the reality of God is beyond words and beyond human understanding.

The image used most frequently in the Bible is that of light. God is the light of his people, his presence dispels darkness. God is compared to the sun rising (Is. 60.1). Perhaps there had been a time when, even in Israel, the power and might of the sun had been seen as the power and light of God. Whatever the origin of the imagery, the idea of God as light remained. Now God as light, or father or mother is not hard to understand even today, provided that we do not take the words literally and become sidetracked into gender questions.

The problem of biblical imagery only becomes acute when it refers to things no longer familiar to us, such as temple worship.

The Old Testament presents particular problems when we attempt to recover the images used to describe God, because the purists in Israel who reformed the temple cult were set against any attempt to depict God in pictorial language. (2 Kings 22–3 describes a reform which removed more than just the pagan images from the temple. Much of what went was the older tradition of Israel itself, but this is not how the reformers wanted it portrayed.) This can be demonstrated most easily by comparing Exodus 24.10 and Deuteronomy 4.12. The Exodus text describes the events on Mount Sinai; the elders saw the God of Israel on his throne, presumably in a vision. This is a vision of God exactly like that seen by Isaiah (Is. 6), Ezekiel (Ezek. 1) and John (Rev. 4). The Deuteronomy text wants none of this, and emphasises that there was only a voice at Sinai. The presence of the LORD was not a vision to inspire them, but a voice giving commands that had to be obeyed.

This tension between the word and vision was also a tension between new and old, between the law-based religion and the temple-based religion. It can be traced all through the Bible; there was always the question of how one was permitted to describe the presence of God. Exodus 33–4 illustrates the problem well; it is a patchwork of ancient materials with all manner of ideas on the subject. The LORD spoke to Moses face to face in the tent (33.11) and yet later in the same chapter

Moses was told that he could not see the face of the LORD and live (33.20). Controversy over the vision continued into the Christian era. Jesus said that the pure in heart would see God (Mt 5.8), that those who had seen him had seen God (Jn 14.9); elsewhere he distinguished between seeing himself and seeing God the Father, implying that the visions of God in the Old Testament had been visions not of the Father but of the Son (Jn 5.37–9). Such texts open up areas of great complexity and importance for understanding Christian origins and only serve to emphasise how much has been lost of the original context and meaning. (I have dealt with them in my earlier book *The Great Angel,* London 1992.)

Fortunately we have been given more than just a list of commandments and stories and the images drawn from the older temple worship survived in Christian tradition as can be seen in the book of Revelation. The people who collected and transmitted the writings which now form our Old Testament favoured the purists and eliminated much of the imagery. The most vivid temple imagery to describe the presence of God is found, as a result, in books which were not included in the Old Testament, even though many of them were known to the first Christians and used by them. To understand what they were really saying when they used temple language, we are very much dependent on these little-known books.

Every religion has its own way of using words and images; it also has its own ritual acts. Within the Christian community, there is sprinkling of holy water; it can be baptism, exorcism — many things. Breaking bread and drinking wine have many meanings, even though they all claim to derive from one event. The ritual acts of the temple are just as difficult to reconstruct; there are several descriptions of what was done, (for example in Leviticus or the Mishnah), but what these actions 'were' is not easy to determine. If we imagine for a moment the disagreements in our own time as to what baptism does or what the bread and wine are, it is hardly surprising that there is so much disagreement over exactly what was done by means of the ancient temple rituals.

The most important of the temple rituals involved the use of blood; it was either smeared or sprinkled and there seems to have been a distinction between the two acts. The one apparently cleansed and the other consecrated but we cannot be sure. One thing is certain; blood represented life not death (Lev. 17.11; Deut. 12.23). The blood rituals were life-giving rituals even though they involved the death of the animal. This must always be borne in mind when reading New Testament texts about the shedding of blood; it was a symbolic giving of life.

These ritual acts did not just represent a healing or a cleansing. In some way they actually inaugurated and brought about whatever it was they represented. This can be seen more clearly by looking at some of the symbolic actions of the prophets, the so-called acted parables. Ahijah, the prophet from Shiloh, tore his cloak into twelve pieces and told Jeroboam to take ten of them. This inaugurated Jeroboam's rebellion (1 Kgs. 11.29–31). Jeremiah smashed the pot and Jerusalem was destroyed (Jer. 19). Jesus broke the bread and his body was broken. In each case the action directly preceded what it represented and in some way brought it about.

Last, there are the buildings. Every place of worship tells something of the beliefs of the worshippers. The shape of the building, the furnishings, even the movements of the worshippers, all combine to produce a picture of the faith. Thus the Orthodox Christians divide their buildings by means of an icon screen bearing pictures of the saints. The screen represents the division between earth and heaven. The bread and wine are brought from heaven to earth as the heavenly food for the people of God. All this is enacted by means of words and movements, with the food being brought through the screen to the people waiting on earth. The Free churches give a different picture of their beliefs. They have a prominent pulpit, to emphasise the place they give to preaching and teaching. Modern churches have been designed, or redesigned, to have a central or nave altar, to show that the Eucharist or Mass has been brought into the centre of the life of God's people. The earlier custom had been to have an altar at the east end of the church, far away from the congregation who could not fail to have detected the distance between themselves and the central ritual of their faith. Moving the altar was not just a rearrangement of the furniture. Such a centralising of the ritual within the life of the community has had the unexpected side-effect of causing an identity crisis for clergy. Involving the laity raised questions about their status and exactly how they differed from the priests. To the outsider, however, all that had changed was the position of the furniture.

The temple in Jerusalem was also a complex symbol. The building itself was surrounded by a series of concentric courtyards, each of which represented holier ground than the one around it. The outer court was the furthest that any non-Jew could go. Then there was the court of the women, which was the limit for women, then the court of Israel, where men could go to take their sacrifices, and finally there was the court of the priests in which there was the great altar and the temple building itself. This was in three parts; the outer porch, then the *hekal* (the equivalent of the nave in a church) and at the west end the *debir*, holy of holies. The grades of holiness continued from the courtyards into the building. Only the priestly classes could enter the building, and only the high priest could enter the holy of holies, once a year on the Day of Atonement.

The temple buildings were a representation of the universe. They were the centre of the ordered creation, the source of its life and stability. The *hekal* represented the Garden of Eden, the created world, and the holy of holies was heaven, the place of the presence of God. 'Represented' is in fact the wrong word to use; the fact that it is necessary to use it in order to make sense to us shows how great is the gulf between their way of thinking and worshipping and ours. Yet it was their language of worship which formed the first expression of the Christian faith, and which we still use. The temple did not represent heaven and earth, it 'was' heaven and earth (on earth as it is in heaven). The priests were the angels; Malachi 2.7 should probably be translated 'the priest… is the angel of the LORD of Hosts'. The high priest was the chief of the angels, the LORD. In the period of the monarchy, the kings had had the role of the high priest; 'a priest for ever after the order of Melchizedek' (Ps. 110.4). The anointed king had 'been' the LORD, the guardian of Israel in the temple rituals. This is the most reasonable explanation of texts such as 'Thy solemn processions are seen, O God, the processions of my God, my King, into the sanctuary' (Ps. 68.24). Eusebius in his *Proof of the Gospel* showed that the early Christians read the psalms in this way; discussing Psalm 45.6–7, he wrote:

> Thy throne, O God, is for ever and ever… Wherefore God, thy God, has anointed thee… So that the Anointer, being the supreme God, is far above the Anointed, he being God in a different sense. And this would be clear to anyone who knew Hebrew.

In other words, he recognised that the royal rituals of the temple when the king had been anointed and addressed as 'God' were the basis for understanding Christian claims about Jesus.

What happened in the temple reflected, 'was', the process of life itself; the annual cycle of seasonal festivals and regular rituals repaired the damage done by sin and renewed the creation. The key figure in the temple rituals was the means whereby life was given to the land and the people. The temple itself guaranteed the prosperity of the land because it enabled the LORD to be in their midst; thus the poor harvests which blighted the return of the exiles to Jerusalem were due, said Haggai, to the temple being in ruins (Hag. 1.9–10)

The furnishings were also symbolic. The great seven branched lamp was the tree of life. It was also the presence of God with his people, his seven eyes or seven spirits (Zech. 4.10; Rev. 4.5). From this we must conclude that God 'was' not One but several in unity, a foreshadowing of the Trinity. The walls of the *hekal* were decorated with palm trees and cherub figures, because it 'was' the Garden of Eden. The holy of holies was separated from the *hekal* by a great curtain woven from scarlet, blue and purple wools and white linen. These four represented the four elements from which it was believed the universe was created: scarlet was fire, blue was air, purple was sea and linen was earth. The curtain hid the holy of holies from the *hekal*; in other words the created universe hid the visible presence of God. Behind the curtain was darkness; by New Testament times the holy of holies was empty, but the memory remained of what it had formerly contained. In the first temple built by Solomon the holy of holies had been the place of the great throne formed by the wings of two huge golden cherubim (1 Chr. 28.18). This had been the throne of the king, but also the throne of the LORD (1 Chr. 29.23), a clear example of how the temple 'was' both on earth and in heaven. The king 'was' both king and LORD. The holy of holies was a place of deep darkness and yet also the place of the throne of light. Those who passed through the curtain passed from earth to heaven or from heaven to earth.

Exodus 28 and 39 describe the vestments of the high priests; Josephus, the first-century historian, was born into a priestly family (*Jewish War* 1.3); he says that the vestments symbolised the created order:

> The high priest's tunic likewise signifies the earth being of linen and its blue the arch of heaven while it recalls the lightnings by the pomegranates, the thunder by the sound of the bells. His upper garment too denotes universal nature which it pleased God to make of four elements. (*Antiquities* III.184)

This tradition was widely known; the Jews of Egypt knew it as can be seen from the *Wisdom of Solomon;*

> For upon his long robe the whole world was depicted and the glories of the fathers were engraved on the four rows of stones and thy majesty on the diadem on his head. (*Wisdom* 18.24)

and from Philo (*Special Laws* I.84–7). The vestments were made from a fourfold fabric as was the curtain itself. The high priest 'was' the LORD. When he passed through the curtain from the holy of holies to the *hekal*, from heaven to earth, he 'was' the LORD coming to his people, robed in the material world ('Veiled in flesh the Godhead see! Hail the incarnate Deity!'). According to a very old text incorporated into Deuteronomy, it was the LORD who came forth to bring judgement and atonement for the land (Deut. 32.43). In ritual enactment, this must have been the high priest coming out of the holy of holies. The Letter to the

Hebrews uses the Greek of this same verse to describe the incarnation, our Lord coming to his people (Heb. 1.6). (See further my *The Gate of Heaven*, London 1991.)

Words, actions and places were used both to express and to realise temple theology. So closely did the words, actions and places interrelate that it is not possible to separate them. Nor is it possible to find a modern equivalent, because any attempt to tamper with the system distorts and, in the end, destroys it. It was this system of temple theology which carried the original Christian message; the New Testament is full of significant and symbolic words, actions and places which, returned to their original context, recover their original meaning.

Chapter Two

The Light

'God is light' wrote St John, 'and in him is no darkness at all' (1 Jn 1.5). Jesus said 'I am the light of the world' (Jn 8.12). Christians are 'children of light' (Eph. 5.8), because they have risen from the dead (Eph. 5.14). They have been 'called out of darkness into his marvellous light' (1 Pet. 2.9), even though 'the King of Kings and Lord of Lords alone has immortality and dwells in unapproachable light' (1 Tim. 6.16). 'The true light came into the world' (Jn 1.9) and this light was also life (Jn 1.4). Light and life, then, are linked and set in opposition to darkness and death. The presence of God is light; coming into the presence of God transforms whatever is dead and gives it life.

These images are so familiar that they are rarely questioned. Light, after all, is something everyone knows. It is easy to find several levels of meaning in such passages, and good sermons can be preached on light and darkness simply by drawing on common experience: light helps us find the way, light is essential if plants are to grow, shadows are cast when something stands in front of the light and so on. All these observations are undoubtedly true, but if this is the only way in which the biblical light passages are read, then the greater part of what they say will not be heard. Beneath the familiar phrases of the New Testament there is a particular set of ideas about light and the process by which light and life were linked. Why were the resurrected called 'children of light'? Why was the light in a particular place where people could go and start a new life? How did all these images fit together and where did they come from in the first place?

The writers of the Dead Sea Scrolls also used the images of light and darkness; the Community Rule describes the community as the sons of light, destined by God to live in the light and to fight against the sons of darkness (1QS III). The War Scroll says that the 'Prince of Light' was to be their helper (1QM XIII); everlasting light would bring them peace and blessing. Perhaps if we had more of their writings we would have even more points of contact with the New Testament. As it is, we have sufficient to see that the Christians were not the only ones to speak in these terms and to describe themselves as the children of light.

The images of light and darkness were rooted in the Old Testament and had been part of the religious language of Israel for many centuries. So much of the New Testament cannot be understood apart from its Old Testament background and the significance of light is perhaps the most outstanding example of this. Isaiah said: 'The people who walked in darkness have seen a great light' (Is. 9.2); 'Arise, shine, for your light has come, And the glory of the LORD has risen upon you' (Is. 60.1). In texts such as these the imagery is drawn from the sunrise, and presents no problems. Sometimes it is made explicit; the LORD is described as the sun: 'The sun of righteousness shall arise, with healing in his wings' (Mal. 4.2); 'The LORD came from Sinai, and dawned from Seir upon us, he shone forth from Mount Paran' (Deut. 33.2). This is more difficult to explain. It may be that there had been times when sun worship was part of the temple rituals, but whether this was really sun worship, or simply too vivid a use of sun imagery cannot be known for certain.

Those responsible for the transmission of the Old Testament were opposed to all forms of imagery and it is unlikely that they would have been sympathetic to anything like sun imagery. Ezekiel saw twenty-five men in the temple, facing the east and worshipping the sun. This was one of the sins for which the temple was destroyed (Ezek. 8.16). Josiah had horses and chariots removed from the temple because they had been dedicated to the sun (2 Kgs. 23.11). The sun worship episode continued as a bitter memory, and each year the prayers at the feast of Tabernacles in the autumn included a solemn declaration: 'Our fathers when they were in this place turned their backs towards the temple of the LORD and their faces toward the east and they worshipped the sun toward the east; but for us, our eyes are turned toward the LORD' (Mishnah *Sukkah* 5.4).

The Qumran community, on the other hand, who were dedicated to maintaining the purity of

Israel's religion, used to face the rising sun every morning and say a morning prayer 'which had been handed down by their fathers' (Josephus, *Jewish War* 2.8.5). All we can say for certain is that there had been a profound disagreement over the imagery which was acceptable to describe the Lord. The Christians kept the sun imagery, as can be seen from Zechariah's song: '… when the day shall dawn upon us from on high, to give light to those who sit in darkness' (Lk 1.78); from Matthew's account of the transfiguration: '… his face shone like the sun' (Mt 17.2); and from John's vision of the Lord in heaven: '… and his face was like the sun shining in full strength' (Rev. 1.16).

Other examples in the Old Testament suggest it was not the sun but a light shining from the holy of holies itself: 'Thou who art enthroned upon the cherubim, shine forth… restore us, O God; let thy face shine that we may be saved' (Ps. 80.1, 3); 'Out of Zion… God shines forth' (Ps. 50.2). It has been suggested that during the great autumn festival in the temple, at the time of the equinox, the sun's light shone through the eastern door of the temple and illuminated the sanctuary. This was held to symbolise the LORD coming to his temple. Ezekiel certainly implies something of the sort when he describes the New Year in the temple (Ezek. 40.1). The glory of the LORD came from the east, entered the temple by the east gate and filled it (Ezek. 43.1–5). In his vision, Ezekiel had been conducted around the temple and he watched as the glory of the LORD returned. The glory, here clearly associated with the sunrise, is described as the great fiery throne of God which he had seen in his earlier vision by the river Chebar (Ezek. 1.4–28). There had been a great fiery cloud in which could be seen the four living creatures and the wheels of the throne. Above them was a sapphire throne on which was seated a being with human form, fiery like molten bronze, and encircled with the brightness of a rainbow.

This linking of the light and the throne of God is the key to understanding the 'light' imagery of the Old Testament. The great source of light, which dawned upon the people like the sunrise, was actually the glory of the presence of the LORD, described by the prophets and visionaries as a burning throne, surrounded by fiery creatures. On earth, i.e. in the temple, this throne was the two giant cherubim in the holy of holies, but in the heavenly scheme of things it was the throne of the glory of God. 'The LORD is in his holy temple' wrote the psalmist, 'the LORD's throne is in heaven' (Ps. 11.4). Jeremiah knew that 'A glorious throne set on high from the beginning is the place of our sanctuary' (Jer. 17.12). Thus the holy of holies, a place of complete darkness in the Jerusalem temple, 'was' a place of burning light which none could approach.

The most detailed description of the holy of holies is found in 2 Chronicles 3.8–14. It was a ten metre cube in shape, overlaid with fine gold, and it was completely filled by two huge cherub statues with outstretched wings. There were upper chambers to the holy of holies (what these were is not known, perhaps niches or shrines for other cherub figures?), and there was a curtain. That is all we know about its physical form. What it 'was' is another matter.

Every time there is a description of the throne, it is a description of the holy of holies. Isaiah saw the throne in his vision; when he was in the temple he saw the LORD and the burning heavenly beings, the seraphim. He said that he had seen 'The King, the LORD of Hosts' (Is. 6.1–8). Ezekiel has more detail. In his vision he saw the glory of the God of Israel in the inner court of the temple (Ezek. 8.4). What follows is a description of how the glory of the LORD left the polluted temple. The scene is clearly the temple but also the heaven of the vision. The man in linen, an angel, is told to take coals from between the cherubim and scatter them on the city. In the temple there was a small incense altar in the *hekal*, in front of the curtain. Vision and reality corresponded. The glory of the LORD went up from the sanctuary in a bright cloud, and the prophet describes in detail how the glory went out from the temple as he knew it. It went to the great door (Ezek. 10.18) and then the cherubim lifted up the throne with their wings and the glory departed.

This, then, was the glory which shone forth from Zion (Ps. 50.2), the shining one enthroned upon the cherubim (Ps. 80.1). When the priests blessed the people, they asked that the face of the LORD would shine on them and give them peace (Num. 6.24–6). Daniel prayed that the LORD would cause his face to shine on his deserted sanctuary (Dan. 9.17). The psalmist prayed that the LORD's face might shine upon him (Pss. 4.6; 31.16). The light was described as a garment, the robe of God's honour and majesty (Ps. 104.2), but it was too bright for mortal eyes. Moses asked to see the glory but was told that no man could see God and live

(Ex. 33.18–20). God covered him and protected him from the glory while he passed by. In the temple, the glory of God was veiled by the great curtain in order to protect human beings from its overwhelming power. 'His brightness,' says Habakkuk, 'was like the light but he veiled his power' (Hab. 3.4).

The most vivid descriptions of the glory are to be found not in the Old Testament but in the other books of the period, those which the rabbis called 'the outside books'. The earliest of these accounts is in *1 Enoch*; nobody knows the age of this material. The number of copies of the book found amongst the Dead Sea Scrolls shows that it was an important text for them. The oldest of the copies is older than any known text of the Bible. This does not mean that *1 Enoch* is older than the Old Testament, but it does mean that, just as we do not give a date to the biblical books on the basis of the oldest fragments of them known to exist, so too we cannot say that the oldest pieces of *1 Enoch* are necessarily evidence for the date when it was first written. We know only that the book with its extraordinary description of the light of God's glory is very old.

The vision described in *1 Enoch* 14 is what Enoch saw when he entered the heavenly temple. The description is such that the actual temple is clearly the setting for the vision, but any attempt to distinguish between earthly and heavenly brings modern distortions to an ancient text. Enoch was carried upwards by clouds and mists, and lightnings bore him into heaven.

Behold in the vision clouds invited me and a mist summoned me, and the course of the stars

and the lightnings sped and hastened me, and
the winds in the vision caused me to fly and
lifted me upwards and bore me into heaven.
And I went in till I drew nigh to a wall which
is built of crystals and surrounded by tongues
of fire: and it began to affright me. And I went
into the tongues of fire and drew nigh to a
large house which was built of crystals: and
the walls of the house were like a tessellated
floor of crystals and its groundwork was of
crystal. Its ceiling was like the path of the stars
and the lightnings and between them were
fiery cherubim, and their heaven was (clear
as) water. A flaming fire surrounded the walls
and its portals blazed with fire. And I entered
into that house, and it was hot as fire and cold
as ice: there were no delights of life therein;
fear covered me and trembling gat hold upon
me. And as I quaked and trembled, I fell upon
my face. And I beheld a vision, And lo! there
was a second house greater than the former,
and the entire portal stood open before me and
it was built of flames of fire. And in every
respect it so excelled in splendour and
magnificence and extent that I cannot describe
to you its splendour and its extent. And its
floor was of fire and above it were lightnings
and the path of the stars and its ceiling also
was flaming fire. And I looked and saw a lofty
throne: its appearance was as crystal and the
wheels thereof as the shining sun and there
was the vision of cherubim. And from
underneath the throne there came streams of
flaming fire so that I could not look thereon.

And the Great Glory sat thereon and his raiment shone more brightly than the sun and was whiter than any snow. None of the angels could enter and could behold his face by reason of the magnificence and glory and no flesh could behold him. Flaming fire was round about him and a great fire stood before him and none around could draw nigh him; ten thousand times ten thousand stood before him yet he needed no counsellor.

(R. H. Charles' translation of *1 Enoch* 14)

No angel could enter his presence, but Enoch was summoned to the gate to hear the message of judgement he had to take to the fallen angels. It is not hard to see here the outer wall of the temple courtyard and the *hekal*. The second house within the first was the golden cube of the holy of holies, the house of fire where he saw the throne of God.

There is another description of the vision in *1 Enoch* 71. Enoch ascended to the heavens and saw the holy sons of God, beings with shining faces and white robes who walked on flames of fire. He saw two fiery streams and then fell prostrate before the Lord of Spirits. The text is somewhat confused, but what follows seems to be a description of the second house surrounded by streams of fire. Ranks of heavenly beings guarded the throne of glory and the four archangels, Michael, Raphael, Gabriel and Phanuel went in and out of the second house.

The Enochic writings seem to have been collected over a period of time. *1 Enoch* 14 is part of the oldest section of the book, and was certainly in existence when Daniel 7 was written. A comparison of the two is important, not least because Daniel 7 was frequently used by the early church to describe the second coming of Jesus. Like *1 Enoch*, Daniel described the great throne of fire with its fiery wheels (Dan. 7.9). The One on the throne was dressed in white and streams of fire came from the foot of the throne. The hosts of heaven stood around. Then Daniel saw a human figure carried upwards by clouds; he was brought into the presence of God and given 'dominion and glory and kingdom' (Dan. 7.14). What is interesting about this chapter is that Daniel does not himself *ascend*; he describes someone else's experience of ascent, a human figure being taken up on clouds. The description in *1 Enoch*, however, is written by someone who had actually had the experience of being taken up in a visionary state to behold the fiery throne. He had been carried by clouds, mists and lightnings into the place of the throne. Perhaps *1 Enoch* contains the visionary experience of one of the ancient high priests. *3 Enoch*, a later book in the same tradition, records the mystical ascent of Rabbi Ishmael, the high priest. (The name Enoch may itself point to this; it means 'the one who has been given knowledge, the consecrated one, the initiated'.)

The first Christians recognised Jesus as the human figure (son of man) of Daniel's vision; Jesus was the one who had entered the place of light and had been given the dominion, glory and kingdom. When Luke describes the Ascension, he says: 'He was lifted up and a cloud took him' (Acts 1.9). This is the viewpoint of the observer. The description of the Transfiguration is similar

(Lk 9.28–36 and parallels). Jesus was also named as the great high priest (Heb. 4.14). According to the Fourth Gospel, however, Jesus speaks as one who has had the experience of ascent to heaven; in the light of what is recorded of the temple mystics, sayings such as 'He bears witness to what he has seen' (Jn 3.32); 'I have come down from heaven' (Jn 6.42); 'I am from above' (Jn 8.23) could be authentic and not, as is so often suggested, the product of the later Christian community. They may be a glimpse of Jesus' own mystical experiences and a clue to his own sense of who he was. (We shall return to this in Chapter 5.)

Among the Dead Sea Scrolls there are some fragments of hymns written in the first century BC, to be sung at the time of the Sabbath sacrifices. Even though so little has survived, the glory and brilliance of the throne were clearly central to their worship:

> From between his glorious wheels there is as it were a fiery vision of most holy spirits. Above them the appearance of rivulets of fire in the likeness of gleaming brass... radiance in many coloured glory... In the midst of a glorious appearance of scarlet they hold to their holy station before the king, spirits of colour in the midst of an appearance of whiteness. (4Q 405)

Other texts show how literally they understood the unity of heaven and earth; those who led the earthly worship were the angels before the heavenly throne. The Master's blessing for the priests was: 'May you be as an Angel of the

Presence in the abode of holiness...'(1QSb 4). Another of their hymns says:

> Thou wilt bring thy glorious salvation to all the men of thy council, to those who share a common lot with the Angels of the Face (1QH 6).

When the First Letter to Timothy spoke of the King of Kings dwelling in unapproachable light (1 Tim. 6.16), Timothy would have known exactly what was meant. He would also have known the correspondence between the earthly and the heavenly which was at the heart of temple worship. The glory of the throne 'was' the holy of holies, the priests 'were' the angels, the ritual acts performed in the temple were part of a cosmic system of healing and restoration. The questions which came so quickly to the Christians who had no Jewish roots such as, 'How could Jesus have been both God and Man?' would not have arisen in the minds of those nurtured in the temple.

Thus it was that the book of Revelation and the Fourth Gospel could both describe Jesus as the light. Revelation has the heavenly aspect, the Gospel the earthly aspect. In Revelation, John learns that the fiery figure on the throne with his flaming eyes and face like the shining sun is the LORD in heaven. But, heaven and earth are one and the same, they cannot be divided, and so the Gospel shows this figure of light as he is on earth. The incarnate LORD was the light shining in the darkness (Jn 1.5) and the glory which even Moses could not look upon had been present on the earth. 'We have beheld his glory' wrote John (Jn 1.14).

Jesus himself said, 'I am the light of the world' (Jn 8.12). When the two worlds coalesced, the disciples were able to see through the veil of the material world and glimpse the reality beyond. 'He was transfigured before them and his face shone like the sun and his garments became white as light' (Mt 17.2). It has often been observed that what changed was not the LORD but the eyes of those who saw him.

When the light shone in the darkness it did not simply illuminate what was there. The coming of the light was the coming of life and the effect of the light was to purify and transform; we shall return to this too in Chapter 5. If for purification and transformation we substitute the words judgement and new creation or death and resurrection, the pieces of the pattern begin to fall into place.

Chapter Three

The Life

'In the beginning, God created the heavens and the earth. The earth was without form and void, and darkness was upon the face of the deep; and the Spirit of God was moving over the face of the waters. And God said, "Let there be light"; and there was light'. This is how the Bible begins, and this is how theology begins, exploring the link between God and this world. Our twentieth-century minds have been so dazzled (I chose that word deliberately!) by increased scientific knowledge that the real meaning of the biblical creation stories has been overshadowed. Darwin and all the controversies surrounding his theory of evolution have managed to dominate any discussions of the creation stories. More recent attempts to explain the ultimate origin of the universe have, as often as not, no need of the hypothesis of a creator. Perhaps the time has come to reclaim the Genesis stories and use them as their authors intended, namely, to show the process by which God relates to the created world.

It should come as no surprise that the Old Testament texts which show how God relates to the created world were originally associated with the temple, the source of life where heaven and earth were joined. There is a lesser known story of the Garden of Eden recorded by Ezekiel who made it quite clear that *his* Garden was a heavenly place (Ezek. 28.12–19). It was not Adam and Eve who were cast out, but a royal figure who was a heavenly being. The present text says he was the king of Tyre but there are indications that he was in fact the king/high priest in Jerusalem, and that the text has changed in transmission. A comparison of the list of gemstones in the Greek of Ezekiel 28.13 and Exodus 28.17–20 shows that the heavenly figure dressed like the high priest. This priest/king had been on the holy mountain of God, walking among the stones of fire. (Some think that should be translated 'sons of fire'). Ezekiel's Garden was the fiery place which others had seen and entered in their vision, for example: 'Who among us can dwell with the devouring fire? Who among us can dwell with the everlasting burnings?... Your eyes will see the king in his beauty, they will behold a land that stretches afar' (Is. 33.14, 17). He was telling of the expulsion of the heavenly aspect of the priest/king which corresponded to the fall of the earthly king and his city. On earth as it is in heaven. It may be that prophetic oracles such as this were a part of the temple rituals; the prophets, like Enoch, had been called to carry the message of judgement on the

fallen angels. This then would be Ezekiel's oracle
on the demise of the monarchy in Jerusalem, and
the fall of the city to the Babylonians. It would
explain the counter-oracles of Isaiah: 'You are my
servant; I have chosen you and not cast you off'
(Is. 41.8). The suffering of the fallen priest/king
was then explained as the suffering of the Servant
of the LORD. The destruction of the temple was
more than just the sacking of a building; it was a
major disturbance in the pattern of the created
order.

We have already seen that the *hekal* represented
the Garden of Eden. The walls were decorated
with figures of cherubim, palm trees and open
flowers (1 Kgs. 6.29). The seven branched lamp
was the tree of life and the tree of life was the place
where the LORD rested when he walked in his
garden (*2 Enoch* 8.3). The fiery throne rested by
the tree when the LORD came as judge (*Apocalypse
of Moses* 22). These later traditions, all current in
the first century AD, are additions to the biblical
story of Eden, but they show that it continued to
be associated with the temple. From the Garden
of Eden flowed a river (Gen. 2.10) which divided
into four and then watered the whole earth. In the
temple visions that same river came from the
throne of God, and so when John had his vision of
heaven he saw the river of life flowing not from
Eden but from the throne of God and out through
the main street of the new Jerusalem (Rev. 22.1–
2).

The rivers flowing from the throne in the
temple had been described by the poets and
visionaries of Israel for centuries. The heavenly

city and the earthly became one; there is no river in the real Jerusalem, and yet the psalmist could write: 'There is a river whose streams make glad the city of God, the holy habitation of the Most High' (Ps. 46.4). The prophets looked forward to the day when heaven and earth would be one; this would follow the Day of Judgement, when the creation would be renewed and restored. Everything that had destroyed the unity of earth and heaven would be removed. After the judgement, wrote the prophet Joel, '... the mountains shall drip sweet wine, and the hills shall flow with milk, and all the stream beds of Judah shall flow with water; and a fountain shall come forth from the house of the LORD and water the valley of Shittim [the Dead Sea valley]' (Joel 3.18). It was a curiously practical vision; the stream beds of Judah did dry up in the summer, and the Dead Sea valley was a barren waste, yet both would be improved by the waters from the temple. Zechariah had a similar hope for the future; on the Day of Judgement, living waters would flow from Jerusalem and continue flowing even in the summer (Zech. 14.8).

Ezekiel gives the most detailed account of the water from the temple. In his vision of the restored temple, the prophet saw a river flowing from under the door of the temple and out through the east gate. As the volume of water increased, so he measured the depth; first it was ankle deep, then knee deep, then it was up to the top of his legs and finally it was too deep to walk through and swimming was the only way to cross. The water flowed through the waterless desert and finally into the Dead Sea where it made the water fresh enough to support a fishing industry. The swamps, however, did not receive fresh water, but remained to provide salt (Ezek. 47.11). Fruit trees grew by the river, bearing a crop every month because the water which irrigated them came from the sanctuary. Their leaves had healing properties. There is something very down-to-earth about these visions; the benefits of the renewed creation would be an increased food supply. Including earth in the vision in this way shows yet again how the temple was the meeting point of heaven and earth, and the waters flowing from it exemplified its role as the source of life.

The imagery, however, was much more subtle than the visions of Zechariah, Joel and Ezekiel suggest, and had we only their accounts of the living water, a great deal would have been lost. First, the water brought life in every sense; Psalm 36, an early psalm, describes the experience of the cherub throne and its river:

> The children of men take refuge in the shadow
>   of thy wings.
> They feast on the abundance of thy house,
> and thou givest drink from the river of thy
>   delights.
> For with thee is the fountain of light;
> and in thy light do we see light. (Ps. 36.7–9)

Here, the water is light, perhaps enlightenment. The visions of Enoch describe a fountain of righteousness which never runs dry, surrounded by fountains of wisdom where the thirsty drink and become wise. Once they have drunk from the fountain, they live with the holy ones (*1 Enoch* 48. 1). Wisdom flows like water and the glory cannot be measured (*1 Enoch* 49.1).

Water as Wisdom is an important element in this symbolism, but unfortunately it is not entirely clear what, or who, was meant by Wisdom. One of the most likely explanations is that Wisdom was a name for the creative power of God, more usually known as the Spirit. Substituting the word Spirit for Wisdom certainly gives a familiar picture: those who drink of the Spirit live with the holy ones i.e. attain the life of heaven. They also become wise. Now Wisdom in the Old Testament was regarded in two very different ways; the reformers were suspicious of Wisdom but the older religion of Israel seems to have recognised that Wisdom i.e. the Spirit, transformed human beings and made them like God. Paul said the same thing in Romans 8.14–17: if the Spirit of God dwells in you, you are sons of God. The serpent in Eden was right; knowledge, that is, Wisdom *did* make human beings god-like. The problem was: was it a good thing for human beings to be god-like, to be sons of God? Those who reformed Israel's religion set themselves against all these ideas, and that is the real root of the difference between Christianity and Judaism. The Christians were not afraid to describe themselves as sons of God.

Again, these ideas of the heavenly stream being Wisdom can be found in the Old Testament, even though we need the later writings to fill in the details. When the kingdom of God is established on earth, wrote Isaiah: 'the earth shall be full of the knowledge of the LORD as the waters cover the sea' (Is. 11.9). After the great judgement described in chapter 34: 'The wilderness and the dry land shall be glad, the desert shall rejoice and blossom;… they shall see the glory of the LORD… for waters shall break forth in the wilderness and streams in the desert' (Is. 35.1–2, 6). The whole creation would be restored: the eyes of the blind would be opened, the ears of the deaf unstopped; the lame man would leap and the dumb sing for joy (Is. 35.5–6). These were the signs of the kingdom of God and this was the evidence offered to John the Baptist when he asked Jesus if he really was the expected Messiah (Lk 7.22). Streams had begun to flow again from the throne, out into the desert of this world. This fulfilled the promise given to Isaiah: 'I will pour water on the thirsty land, and streams on the dry ground; I will pour my spirit on your descendants, and my blessing on your offspring (Is. 44.3). In the Fourth Gospel this link of water and Spirit is made explicit:

> Jesus stood up and proclaimed, 'If anyone thirst, let him come to me and drink. He who believes in me, as the scripture has said, "Out of his heart shall flow rivers of living water."' Now this he said about the Spirit… (Jn 7.37–8)

The rivers from the throne, however, were not simply water; Daniel alone of the biblical writers mentions that the stream was fire (Dan. 7.10) and yet this is made clear in Enoch's visions: 'And from underneath the throne came streams of flaming fire so that I could not look thereon

(*1 Enoch* 14.19); 'And I saw two streams of fire, and the light of that fire shone like hyacinth, and I fell on my face before the Lord of Spirits... On its [the second house] four sides were streams full of living fire' (*1 Enoch* 71.2, 6). *3 Enoch*, although a later compilation of traditions about the throne, adds an interesting detail about the fiery stream: 'The river of fire rises and it flows out from beneath the throne of Glory... and all the ministering angels... go down into the river of fire... and dip their tongues and their mouths' (*3 Enoch* 36); an echo perhaps of Isaiah's experience when his lips were purified by fire brought by the angel (Is. 6.6–7). The river which flowed from the throne of God was both water and fire; it could transform the creation by bringing water to desert places, or it could bring the fire of purifying judgement. One stream, but very different effects. One of the Qumran hymns puts it well:

> A source of light shall become an ever flowing fountain,
> and in its bright flames all the [sons of iniquity] shall be consumed;
> [it shall be] a fire to devour all sinful men in utter destruction. (1QH 6)

The stream from the throne transformed and renewed the creation; judgement was a part of the process.

What then of the original creation? We now return to the account in Genesis 1, to see if there is any difference between the 'first' creation and the renewal and restoration of creation which was depicted in/brought about by temple worship. Genesis 1 does not describe a creation out of nothing. It is one of the commonest misreadings of the text to think that it does. It describes the ordering and transforming of an existing chaos. The word translated 'created' is a Hebrew word only used to describe the activity of God. Whatever this transforming process is, it is not done by human beings. Perhaps 'create' is not an appropriate translation; but what could be? Nor is it an act done once for all and completed; the six-day scheme in Genesis 1 has led to a traditional view of the creation as a task completed and then left, but this is not the biblical view. The creation was constantly sustained by the inflowing Spirit (often translated 'breath') of God. Compare what Jesus said when he had healed the man by the pool of Bethsaida: 'My Father is working still, and I am working' (Jn 5.17). The seventh day of rest was yet to come. The Spirit *was* the life of creation: 'If he should take back his spirit to himself and gather to himself his breath, all flesh would perish together, and man would return to dust' (Job 34.14–15). Thus spoke Elihu, the fourth of those who tried to explain Job's sufferings. He knew that, apart from the Spirit, he was dust: 'The spirit of God has made me, and the breath of the Almighty gives me life' (Job 33.4). This is very similar to the creation of Adam: 'The LORD God formed man of dust from the ground and breathed into his nostrils the breath of life; and man became a living being' (Gen. 2.7). The flowing of life into the creation was the flowing of the Spirit. The sons of God, those who had the Spirit, were to renew and release creation from its decline into decay (Rom. 8.19–21).

When Genesis 1 was read in the first century AD it was read in this way, but with one addition. The agent of the creation was not God but the Son, also called the Word or Wisdom or Spirit. Although there is considerable debate as to exactly how these four relate, Son, Word, Wisdom and Spirit were all sufficiently similar that, for the purposes of a brief introduction such as this, they can be considered equivalents. (The fact that Son and Word are masculine and Wisdom and Spirit are feminine is only a problem for those who wish it to be so.) The Aramaic version of Genesis, which is thought to be the oldest we have giving the traditions of Palestinian Jews, translates the opening verses of Genesis thus:

> From the beginning with Wisdom the Son of the LORD perfected [not created!] the heavens and the earth. And the earth was empty and without form, and desolate without a son of man or beast and void of all cultivation of plants and of trees, and darkness was spread over the face of the abyss and a spirit of love from before the LORD was blowing over the face of the waters. And the Word of the LORD said: Let there be light and there was light according to the decree of his Word. (Targum *Neofiti*: Gen. 1.1–3)

This account of the creation is not unique; Proverbs describes how the LORD was not alone but had a helper, Wisdom.

> The LORD created me at the beginning of his
>   work the first of his acts of old...
> When he established the heavens I was there...
> when he marked out the foundations of the
>   earth,
> then I was beside him like a master workman...
>   (Prov. 8.22, 27, 29–30)

John begins his Gospel with an account of the creation; the Word was the agent:

> In the beginning was the Word and the Word
> was with God and the Word was God. He was
> in the beginning with God; all things were
> made by him and without him was not
> anything made that was made. In him was life
> and the life was the life of men. (Jn 1.1–4)

The creating power of the Word, the creating power of the Spirit, or Wisdom, or the Son was the means whereby the creation was first ordered but the streams from the throne had become impeded. This was expressed in various ways. One story told how Adam and Eve were driven from the Garden to a place of dust and thorns (Gen. 3.17–19), where, unlike the heavenly waters, their own labour could transform nothing; they would eventually return to the dust they had been cultivating. Another told how the Spirit which gave life was withdrawn after the sin of the fallen angels (Gen. 6.3). The process of decline and decay had set in. The prophet Joel shows what the renewed creation would be like. He probably gave his oracles at a time of national disasters, when his people needed reminding of the hope of renewal. The picture is familiar: food supplies increase, rain falls and locusts disappear, and all this is proof that the LORD is in the midst of his people (Joel 2.18–27). 'And it shall come to pass afterwards that I will pour out my spirit on all flesh' (Joel 2.28).

The rivers flow from the throne and life is renewed. Creation is a continuous process not an action completed once for all in the distant past, and life, like the rivers, cannot stand still; change and growth, healing and renewal are signs that the river is still flowing, fire to some, water to others. Those through whom (not *to* whom) the rivers flow are the means of healing and renewal, not only for individuals but for the whole earth. Ezekiel and Zechariah saw rivers flowing from the temple as a source of water, literally, for their barren land. Until the temple was rebuilt, as Haggai knew well, there could be no real prosperity for the land. 'You have looked for much, and, lo, it came to little;... Why? says the LORD of hosts. Because of my house that lies in ruins, while you busy yourselves each with his own house' (Hag. 1.9). This is no quaint relic of ancient fertility beliefs that happens to have survived in the Old Testament; it is a simple statement of what the temple was and did; is and does.

The twentieth century has seen a change in Christian thinking about the creation, now known as Green Theology. The 'finished perfection' of eighteenth-century thinkers was dealt a severe blow by theories of evolution which described not an original perfection ruined by human sin, but rather a struggle to adapt and survive. The Green movement of the late 60s was loud in its criticism of Christians, particularly Protestant Christians, who had understood Genesis 1 as God's command to rule the earth which had been created for their pleasure and convenience. Gradually the emphasis has moved back to a 'Wisdom' theology derived from the thought world of the temple (although it has not been recognised as temple theology!). The Spirit is constantly at work renewing, restoring and recreating; this is a sacramental view of the creation. The themes are now healing and harmony rather than death and dominion. Pierre Teilhard de Chardin was moving towards this in his writing in the first half of this century; he was not well received by the 'establishment'. More recently, Matthew Fox has been exploring another aspect of Wisdom theology, his 'original blessing'; this too has been viewed with alarm by the 'establishment'. Healing and harmony make hierarchy redundant. Feminists such as Rosemary Radford Ruether are presently making a major contribution: 'ecofeminism'. It is all too easy to dismiss this new thinking because it has not been fully worked out; it has rough edges and bad patches here and there, but to dismiss it as 'New Age' and therefore suspect is short-sighted. 'New Age' has become both a convenient label and a reason for ignoring and even condemning it. This is a great loss. New Age (our New Age, that is!) has been fundamental to Christian thinking from the beginning as can be seen from Revelation 21.1: 'A new heaven and a new earth' with the river of life flowing from the throne of God. It would be good to see the Spirit-filled churches of our time at the fighting edge of protest against pollution and crimes against the creation.

All these temple images can work on several levels; the renewing Spirit which flows from the throne can transform the creation on a grand scale, or it can recreate an individual life. The original atonement was a rite of healing for the whole creation. When the Aramaic version of Genesis was made, one very important piece of information was included. The creating Spirit of the LORD which moved over the chaos was the Spirit of love.

Chapter Four

The Blood

Then he shall kill the goat of the sin offering which is for the people, and bring its blood within the veil, and do with its blood as he did with the blood of the bull, sprinkling it upon the mercy seat and before the mercy seat; thus he shall make atonement for the holy place, because of the uncleannesses of the people of Israel, and because of the transgressions, all their sins; and so he shall do for the tent of meeting which abides with them in the midst of their uncleannesses. There shall be no man in the tent of meeting when he enters to make atonement for the holy place until he comes out and has made atonement for himself and for his house and for all the assembly of Israel. Then he shall go out to the altar which is before the LORD and make atonement for it, and shall take some of the blood of the bull and of the blood of the goat and put it on the horns of the altar round about. And he shall sprinkle some of the blood upon it with his finger seven times, and cleanse it and hallow it from the uncleannesses of the people of Israel. (Lev. 16.15–19)

The rituals for the Day of Atonement, as described here in Leviticus, were the most ancient and mysterious in the whole of Israel's religion. This was the only occasion in the year when the high priest entered alone into the holy of holies. He carried with him first a firepan of incense and then a bowl of blood which he sprinkled on the *kapporeth*. The whole occasion was a time of awe; he did not prolong his prayers says the Mishnah '... lest he put Israel in terror' (m. *Yoma* 5.1). The words 'there shall be no man with him when he enters to make atonement' were understood by Philo as 'when he enters to make atonement he shall not be a man' (*On Dreams* II.189, 231), and this is certainly how his actions would have been understood. The high priest, insofar as he was passing into the presence of God, was passing into heaven to serve with the angels. He did not wear his multicoloured vestments on that day, but white linen, the dress of angels.

The origin of the Day of Atonement rituals is lost in antiquity and yet they remained the most important ceremony of the temple year. Two goats were involved; one was chosen by lot 'for the LORD' and the other was chosen 'for Azazel'. Even the meaning of the names is lost; who or what was Azazel? The obvious answer would be that this was the leader of the fallen angels since this was one of his names in later writings such as *1 Enoch*. But why, then, should Azazel be paired with the

LORD, and why should an offering be sent to him? This problem was well-known to rabbis in the early Christian period, some of whom explained that the name actually meant 'rocky place' ('one goat for a rocky place') because the goat was sent out into the desert to a rocky place, the ritual for bearing away the sins of Israel. This seems to be a suggestion devised to fill an awkward gap. Others, however, remembered that Azazel was the fallen angel.

The blood of the goat 'for the LORD' was taken into the holy place. The account in Leviticus describes the rituals as they would have been in the desert, with the tent and the altar in front of it, but they reflect the customs of the Second Temple period. The blood was taken into the holy of holies and sprinkled on the *kapporeth* ('mercy seat' is the usual translation but probably not a good one. The word means the 'place of atonement', but since the meaning of atonement is not clear either, *kapporeth* had better remain untranslated). Then it was brought out and sprinkled in the tent of meeting, and finally it was put on the altar outside. All we are told is that this atoned these places. It is the *places* which are atoned, not the people. The high priest performed the ritual on behalf of, or for himself, his household or the people. But it is not the people who are affected by it; the sense of the text seems to be that the places in the temple had been polluted by the actions of the people, and that the places had to be restored perhaps so that the LORD could dwell there with his people. When the atonement ritual was performed in the temple, the high priest took blood into the places appropriate to the sin which had been committed; first he sprinkled blood in the holy of holies, then on the curtain and then on the golden incense altar in the *hekal*. Any blood which remained was poured at the base of the great altar outside in the courtyard.

The corresponding heavenly aspect of entering the holy of holies is found in the visions of such texts as *1 Enoch*. Like the high priest, Enoch was terrified 'prostrate on his face and trembling' (*1 Enoch* 14.24). He was told to take a message of judgement to the fallen angels. In another account of a vision, Enoch 'fell on his face before the Lord of Spirits' (*1 Enoch* 71.2). *2 Enoch* is similar: 'They placed me at the edge of heaven, alone. And I became terrified; I fell on my face' (*2 Enoch* 21). *3 Enoch* is particularly interesting in this respect. It claims to be the work of one Rabbi Ishmael, the high priest and the Babylonian Talmud gives the additional information that he had had a vision of the Lord in the holy of holies (b. *Berakoth* 7a).

What was the high priest doing on the Day of Atonement? The description of the ritual in Leviticus and the Mishnah is only a description. The Mishnah says exactly how and where the blood was to be sprinkled, once upwards, seven times downwards, and so on, but there is no indication of what the ritual was. It atoned... but that word only means covered, it describes the action. What did it all represent, or, in the thought forms of the temple, what did it correspond to in heaven? What did it do? The problem here is very like the problem someone from another faith might have in trying to understand what is done by Christians with bread and wine. Those who take part know there is a basic story which we remember and then... then the disagreements start. Is it a memorial meal, is it a sacrifice? Is the bread just bread or is it something more? It is quite possible that there were comparable dis-agreements about atonement and the blood.

The atonement rituals seem to have had a similarly controversial history. Whoever wrote Exodus 32 cannot have been sympathetic to the temple cult. After the sin of the golden calf, Moses went up the mountain again to see if he could make atonement for the people's sin. He even offered his own life, but the LORD refused. Those who sinned had to bear the consequences of their sin. No atonement mediated by another was possible. As a result, a plague came on the sinners (Ex. 32.30–5). The very fact that such a story is recorded in the Old Testament shows that there were some people, (possibly even those who compiled the Old Testament?) who were hostile to the theology of atonement. This would certainly explain why it is so hard to reconstruct the origin and meaning of the greatest temple ritual and why there are no clear references to atonement ritual in the histories of the first temple.

The meaning of the blood ritual, and therefore of the whole idea of atonement, has to be deduced as best we can from such evidence as has survived. First, the blood in atonement rituals was said to be life not death and it was the life which atoned. 'For the life of the flesh is in the blood; and I have given it for you upon the altar to make atonement for your souls for it is the blood that makes atonement by reason of the life' (Lev. 17.11). Leviticus again, but the text here is obscure; it has few words, and how they are translated depends very much on what the translator thinks they meant in the first place. 'Life' and 'soul' in this text are the same word, *nephesh*; this implies some similarity or parallel symbolism of the life of the victim and the life of the people, perhaps substitution as has often been suggested, but the emphasis is on the *life* which is used to do something to the holy places.

Second, the atonement ritual purified and hallowed the temple places from the uncleannesses of the people even though these were places where the people themselves were not allowed to go. There cannot have been any idea, then, of direct defilement, bringing an unclean person or object into a holy place. It seems as though we have to read this text in the light of what the temple buildings represented, 'were'. They were the heaven and earth: the place of God's throne, the Garden and the rest of creation outside the Garden. Blood/life was daubed and sprinkled in the places which were the presence of God and the created world, to remove the effects of sin. Atonement, in other words, restored the creation from the effects of human action by means of blood/life. It was the renewal of creation.

Third, the movement of the ritual was outwards from the holy of holies into the world: first the *kapporeth* was sprinkled, then the curtain, then the altar. It was a God-centred ritual. Blood/life was brought from the presence of God to remove the effects of human sin from the world. But whose blood? It was the blood of a goat drawn by lot 'for the LORD'. There were other offerings made in the temple to deal with the effects of sin; but on no other occasion was the animal in question said to be 'for the LORD'. On no other occasion was the blood taken into the holy of holies. There must have been something about blood going into the presence of the LORD which made it necessary to specify that this goat was 'for the LORD'. We shall return to this problem.

It is widely agreed that the three autumn festivals of the post-exilic period, (New Year, Day of Atonement and Tabernacles) were derived from an earlier royal festival held every autumn to celebrate the renewal of the year and the enthronement of the king. Nothing can be proved, but Isaiah 40–55 is thought to be based on the liturgies of this festival and there are many Psalms (e.g. 47, 93, and 95–100, the ones originally suggested by S. Mowinckel) which must have had such a festival as their original setting. It is known that there were elaborate royal rites in the Babylonian New Year festival; the problem is dating the texts. The accounts which survive are from the Seleucid period, but they are copies of older texts. It is quite possible that the same rituals had been performed for centuries and that something very similar was done by contemporaries of Isaiah. The festival celebrated the supreme kingship of Marduk and his power as the creator; the temple was purified by priests using water, incense and incantations. They also 'atoned' the temple building using the decapitated body of a ram which 'absorbed' the impurities and was then thrown into the river. The king was later brought to the temple, stripped of his regalia, ritually beaten and dragged before the god to declare that he had not neglected his duties as king. He was then given his regalia again and struck on the cheek; if the blow brought tears it was a good omen. (The most accessible account of the rituals can be found in J. H. Eaton *Kingship and the Psalms* London 1976, pp. 87, 96; translations of the original texts in J. B. Pritchard *Ancient Near Eastern Texts* Princeton 1955, pp. 331–4.)

Perhaps something similar had happened in Jerusalem? The original rite of atonement would then have been performed by the king; how, we do not know, but the mysterious Suffering Servant depicted in Isaiah 52.13–53.12 was performing an atonement ritual and he seems to have been a royal figure. This Servant Song inspired one of the earliest interpretations of the crucifixion, Philippians 2.5–11. The phrase 'emptied himself' (Phil. 2.7) is the Greek equivalent of the Hebrew 'he makes his soul a sin offering' in Isaiah 53.10, since the process of making a sin offering was to pour out the blood/life, and 'his soul' in Isaiah means 'himself'. In Philippians the Servant figure is then exalted to receive homage and is given royal status. It is possible, of course, that this sequence of atonement and enthronement was invented by the first Christians, but given that they preached fulfilment of the scriptures, and attributed to Jesus the belief that he had suffered to enter glory in fulfilment of the scriptures (Lk 24.26–7; what scriptures, we may ask?), the Christian evidence in Philippians may be evidence not only for the pattern of the ancient atonement but also for to its being known as late as the first century AD.

There is a curious text in *1 Enoch* which may be further evidence. The second section of the book is known as the Similitudes or Parables; it is the only section of *1 Enoch* not identified at Qumran and there is no proof that it is pre-Christian. The Parables are three visions of a heavenly Man figure enthroned for the Day of Judgement. The simple process of matching words and phrases shows that this Man figure was Isaiah's Servant of the Lord; but the Parables reveal more of his role than do Isaiah's Servant Songs. In *1 Enoch* 46 the Man ascends to heaven in the manner of Daniel's vision (Dan. 7.9–14), an important text for the early church, and the purpose of his exaltation is described in language reminiscent of the Magnificat (Lk 1.46–55). Then the prayers of the righteous ones and the blood of the Righteous One are brought into the presence of the Ancient of Days, the books are opened and the judgement begins (*1 Enoch* 47). The text is a problem here, with a mixture of singular and plural; one cannot but be reminded of John's Revelation: it is the Lamb by the throne, standing as though it has been slain, which opens the books of judgement (Rev. 5.7); but in Aramaic, Lamb and Servant are the same word, *talya'*! Revelation seems to be describing this same rite of atonement, with the Servant going into the heavenly temple.

The original temple rites were heaven on earth, and the king was the LORD. The Chronicler says that Solomon sat on the throne of the LORD as king

(1 Chr. 29.23); perhaps the psalms which celebrated the enthronement of the LORD were describing rites for the Davidic king who 'was' the LORD. If the king performed the atonement rites, (and we cannot begin to guess exactly what was done), the goat's blood 'for the LORD' must have been the equivalent rite in the later period.

The blood of the goat 'for the LORD' was taken into the holy of holies and sprinkled on the *kapporeth*. According to the desert tradition, the LORD spoke to Moses from above the *kapporeth*, between the cherubim (Ex. 25.22; Num. 7.89). According to the temple tradition, the LORD was enthroned upon the cherubim (Pss. 80.1; 99.1). It would seem that the *kapporeth* of the desert tradition was equivalent to the throne in the temple tradition, the throne which was in itself divine. Psalm 45.6 is an unclear text; addressed to the king, it could be saying 'Your divine throne endures for ever' or, 'Your throne, O God, endures for ever' or even 'Your throne is God for ever'. We have no means of deciding between the possibilities, but an ancient Egyptian custom, in use as late as the time of the Davidic kings in Jerusalem, may be relevant. The royal insignia were believed to carry the divine power, especially the throne which was believed to be the source of the king's divinity. The throne was Isis, and the king was described as her son. (See H. Frankfort, *Kingship and the Gods* London and Chicago 1948, 1962, pp. 43–4.)

If, and it is a big if, there had been some similar belief in Jerusalem, then the throne would have been the presence of the LORD and the king would have become the divine son at his enthronement. This is what Psalm 2.6–7 and Psalm 110 imply, especially the Greek version of Psalm 110.3 which reads 'Today I have begotten you'. Such a belief would explain the difficulties both of Psalm 45.6 which suggests that the throne was divine and also of Romans 3.23, which describes Jesus as the new *kapporeth*. (The Greek word *hilasterion* used here translates *kapporeth* in the Septuagint Greek of Exodus 25 and means the *kapporeth* in Hebrews 9.5 also.) It would be odd if Paul had compared Jesus to a piece of temple furniture, but had he known the original significance of the *kapporeth*, that it 'was' the divine presence, then his comparison would have been apt. Whatever the *kapporeth* was, the blood was brought there first in the rituals and then taken out into the rest of the temple.

All rituals have an accompanying story which they re-enact; the bread and wine ritual in the church has the Last Supper, the Jewish Passover has the Exodus from Egypt and so on. It seems that the Day of Atonement was the Day of Judgement, the Day of the LORD. There are many graphic accounts of the judgement, describing its heavenly aspect. Isaiah 34, for example, describes the Day of the LORD'S vengeance which precedes the establishment of the new creation. Habakkuk 3 describes the LORD coming from his holy mountain as a warrior. The psalmist hints that the judgement took place in the temple; when he was overwhelmed by the wickedness of his enemies and their apparent prosperity, he admitted that he could make no sense of it:

But when I thought how to understand this,
it seemed to me a wearisome task, until I went
into the sanctuary of God; then I perceived
their end. (Ps. 73.16–17)

Isaiah, too, expected the Lord to come from the
temple on the Day of Judgement:

Hark an uproar from the city! A voice from
the temple!

The voice of the LORD rendering recompense
to his enemies. (Is. 66.6)

John's Revelation is the most detailed account in
the Bible; again, it is set in the temple, with the
throne, the seven branched lamp, the altar of
incense and the angels/priests offering prayers
(Rev. 8.3). Such pictures of fury and violence,
especially in the New Testament which is clearly
a Christian book, have been the cause of great
concern and are often neglected as a result. They
describe the fire aspect of the streams from the
throne, the destruction of evil. But there was also
the water, the healing and positive side: Isaiah 61
describes someone anointed to bring good news
to the afflicted and liberty to captives; this, he says,
is to be the time of the Lord's favour and the Day
of God's vengeance. Fire and water at the same
time. This was the passage read by Jesus when he
began his ministry in the Nazareth synagogue;
'Today this scripture has been fulfilled in your
hearing' (Lk 4.21). Jesus saw himself as
inaugurating the Day of the LORD, the judgement
and the new creation.

The non-biblical books give more details of the
heavenly aspect of the Day of the LORD and they go

a long way towards explaining what was intended by the Day of Atonement rituals. *1 Enoch* has several accounts of the Day: this is part of the oldest:

> The LORD said to Raphael: 'Bind Azazel hand and foot, and cast him into the darkness: and make an opening in the desert which is in Dudael, and cast him therein. And place upon him rough and jagged rocks and cover him with darkness and let him abide there forever and cover his face that he may not see the light. And on the great day of judgement he shall be cast into the fire. Heal the earth which the angels have corrupted and proclaim the healing of the earth, *that they may heal the plague* and that the children of men may not perish...' (*1 Enoch* 10.4–7).

As so often happens with ancient texts that have survived in different forms and different languages, there are other possibilities for some words. One is that the italicised words should be 'that I may heal the earth'. Once Azazel has been cast out, the LORD could heal the earth. Azazel was cast out because the whole earth had been corrupted by what he taught: 'Write upon him all sin' (*1 Enoch* 10.8). (The nature of Azazel's fate should not pass without comment; he is cast out, rather than destroyed or subjected to some other punishment. Under one or other of his many names, Azazel's expulsion appears in the New Testament at Luke 10.18, Satan falls like lightning; John 12.31, the ruler of this world is cast out; and Revelation 12.9, the ancient serpent called the devil and Satan thrown down from heaven.)

Later writings about the Day of Atonement show that the place where Azazel was imprisoned, the rough and jagged rocks of Dudael, was the place to which the goat 'for Azazel' was sent. The Mishnah says the goat was sent to Beth Hiddudo (m. *Yoma* 6.8) and an Aramaic version of Leviticus says it went to Beth Hadure (T. *Pseudo-Jonathan* on Leviticus 16.21). (Given the possibilities of misreading Hebrew letters, the Dudael of *1 Enoch* seems to be the same place.) If the goat 'for Azazel' in Leviticus was the banishing of Azazel to the desert place in *1 Enoch,* and if the Targum says that the goat was killed in the desert whereas *1 Enoch* says it was Azazel who perished we must conclude that *1 Enoch* gives the myth and Leviticus the rituals for the Day of Atonement. The blood ritual in the temple, with the high priest coming out of the holy of holies, must have been the 'healing of the earth'.

There are several biblical passages which describe how the LORD came from his holy of holies for the judgement: 'For behold the LORD is coming forth out of his place to punish the inhabitants of the earth for their iniquity, and the earth will disclose the blood shed upon her, and will no more cover her slain' (Is. 26.21). 'For behold the LORD is coming forth out of his place, and will come down and tread upon the high places of the earth. And the mountains will melt under him and the valleys be cleft like wax before the fire, like waters poured down a steep place' (Mic. 1.3). It is an ancient text embedded in Deuteronomy which tells us what the LORD was *doing* when he came from his holy place:

He avenges the blood of his servants,
and takes vengeance on his adversaries,
and atones the land of his people. (Deut. 32.43)

This must be what the Enochic text described as
the 'healing of the earth'. Atonement was seen as
healing the wounds caused in the creation by the
conduct either of the fallen angels, or of their
human counterparts. *1 Enoch* itself begins with a
description of the LORD coming forth from his holy
place: 'The great Holy One will come forth from
his dwelling,… And there shall be judgement on
all men, (*1 Enoch* 1.1, 8). There follows the
description of the fallen angels and the binding of
Azazel.

Who, then, 'was' the high priest who performed
the blood ritual? 'On earth as it is in heaven'; he
must have been the LORD. There are several
grounds for thinking this. The first is the system
of correspondences in temple rituals; someone
must have had this role. Second, we know that
the high priest wore the divine name on his
forehead. The reformed Old Testament is rather
sensitive about this and says that he wore a plate
of gold on the front of his turban which said 'Holy
to the LORD' (Ex. 28.36) but other ancient texts say
that the golden plate was inscribed simply with
the four letters of the sacred name. When he wore
the sacred name he was able to make atonement
(b. *Yoma* 7a). Third, one of the Dead Sea texts
describes the great Day of Atonement when a
heavenly high priest, Melchizedek, will atone for
the children of light and bring judgement on Satan.
This Melchizedek is described as your God (11Q
Melch).

If the goat 'for Azazel' was the banished Azazel, sent off to his prison in the desert, the goat 'for the LORD' must have represented the LORD. The animal's life was a substitute for the life of the LORD. When the high priest carried the blood/life of the 'goat for the LORD' into the holy place he was carrying the 'life' of the LORD, a substitute for himself. Then he came out to atone the holy place, to heal the earth. The high priest, the LORD, brought about the healing and renewal by absorbing the effects of the evil into himself. Again, this has to be deduced from several texts: the high priest absorbed ('bore') the impurities of the people's offerings when he was wearing the golden plate of the sacred name (Ex. 28.38); the Suffering Servant made atonement when he bore the sins and iniquities of many (Is. 53.11–12); Jesus the healer 'bore' infirmities and diseases of those he cured (Mt 8.17). Having absorbed all the impurities into himself, the high priest transferred them to the head of the goat 'for Azazel' and sent them into the desert. How could he have transferred the sins unless they were 'his' to transfer? (**NB** The Hebrew word *nasa'* means both 'bear' and 'forgive'.)

All this is a tentative reconstruction based on the pieces of evidence which happen to have survived. It does, however, make sense of the otherwise obscure illustrations offered in the Letter to the Hebrews.

But when Christ appeared as a high priest of the good things that have come, then through the greater and more perfect tent (not made with hands, that is, not of this creation) he entered once for all into the holy place, taking

not the blood of goats and bulls but his own
blood thus securing an eternal redemption.
(Heb. 9.11–12)

The parallel is pressed further when Jesus' death
outside the city walls is compared to disposing of
the goat's body; after the blood had been used in
the ritual the carcase was burned outside the camp
(Heb. 13.11–12). If the argument of these passages
is to have any meaning it must be that the death
of Jesus was the final Day of Atonement offering,
not the annual temple substitutes when the LORD
and his Day had been ritualised, but the heavenly
reality realised. The LORD had come and made the
great atonement where there was no substitution.
Jesus had already been named as Melchizedek, the
great high priest, and Deuteronomy 32.43,
describing the LORD'S coming to judge and atone,
had already been used in the opening sequence of
quotations; Hebrews 1.6 quotes the Greek form of
the verse.

   The life and healing which came from the
temple, then, was described in two ways; it was
the stream which flowed from the throne, or it was
the blood which was brought from the throne.
Both images were used of Jesus. John spoke of
Jesus' body as the temple (Jn 2.21) and at the
moment of his death, it is John who records that
he gave up his spirit (Jn 19.30) and that there came
from his side water and blood (Jn 19.34). This
probably explains the enigmatic statement in 1
John 5.6: 'This is the one who comes through [by
means of] water and blood'. The Good News Bible
inserts extra words, at this point which alter the
meaning: it has 'Jesus Christ is the one who *came*

with the water *of his baptism* and the blood *of his death'*. (In the Greek, 'came' is 'comes', a present act not a past event, and the words for 'his baptism' and 'his death' are not there at all.) John here is referring to the three ways in which the power and presence of God come to his people; by the Spirit at creation, by the stream from the throne and by the blood of the Day of Atonement. It is clear from the differences between various ancient versions of this passage that it has puzzled people for a long time. The Authorized Version has verses 7–8 thus:

> For there are three that bear record in heaven, the Father, the Word and the Holy Ghost: and these three are one. And there are three that bear witness in earth: the Spirit and the water and the blood: and these three agree in one.

This translation is based on one version of the Greek. An old Latin text has something similar:

> Spirit, water and blood are witnesses on earth and these three are one in Christ Jesus, and there are three which bear witness in heaven, the Father, the Son and the Spirit.

The emphasis was on the unity of water, blood and Spirit, the ways in which God came into the world. The result of the coming was the same, no matter which piece of symbolism was used: the water restored the earth, the Spirit recreated the earth, the blood/life healed the earth.

This resulted in a New Covenant. The Old Testament is full of references to covenants, but none except Jeremiah 31.31–7 (a 'cosmic covenant' passage) deals with sin and none could possibly explain the words at the Last Supper 'This is my blood of the new covenant which is poured out for many for the forgiveness of sins (Mt 26.28). Now the word rendered 'forgiveness' means literally 'sending away, getting rid of', and one cannot but be reminded of the goat sent into the desert, bearing the sins. Hebrews explains that Jesus is the mediator of a new covenant because he has made the great atonement (Heb. 9.15). Was the blood rite at the Day of Atonement, which rid the temple of sin, a covenant rite and was this what Jesus had in mind at the Last Supper? There certainly was a priests' covenant in the Old Testament of which very little is known. It was given to Phineas (Num. 25.12–13) and was described as 'the covenant of perpetual priesthood, the covenant of my peace'. Isaiah looked forward to a 'covenant of peace which shall not be removed' (Is. 54.10). Ezekiel the priest prophesied: 'I will make a covenant of peace with them; it shall be an everlasting covenant with them; and I will bless them and multiply them and will set my sanctuary in the midst of them for evermore. My dwelling shall be with them' (Ezek. 37.26). Malachi condemned the priests of his time and compared them with Levi, their ancestor: 'My covenant with him was a covenant of life and peace and I gave them to him that he might fear; and he feared me, he stood in awe of my name' (Mal. 2.5). Why was the covenant given to the priests? Because, says Numbers 25.13, they made atonement.

If we return now to Enoch's vision, the pieces begin to fit together: standing before the throne of the Ancient of Days, Enoch is told by the angel

'He proclaims to thee peace in the name of the world to come; for from hence has proceeded peace since the creation of the world, and so it shall be for ever and ever' (*1 Enoch* 71.15). Paul speaks of this; he calls it the ministry of reconciliation, the work of healing which is the sign of the new covenant. The bond between heaven and earth had been renewed, and thus the wounds of the creation could be healed.

> Therefore if anyone is in Christ he is a new creation; the old has passed away, behold the new has come. All this is from God, who through Christ reconciled us to himself and gave us the ministry of reconciliation; that is, in Christ God was reconciling the world to himself, not counting their trespasses against them, and entrusting to us the message of reconciliation (2 Cor. 5.17–19).

The implication of what Paul says is that all now function as high priests, all have access to the holy of holies and all are the agents of the new covenant. As St Francis put it: 'Make me a channel of your peace.'

The high priesthood of all is the final link in this chain of imagery. Peter describes believers as 'a chosen race, a royal priesthood, a holy nation, God's own people, that you may declare the wonderful deeds of him who called you out of darkness into his marvellous light' (1 Pet. 2.9). And then echoing the experience of the ancient visionaries there is the prayer in the liturgy attributed to St James:

We thank thee, O Lord our God, that thou hast given us boldness for the entrance of thy holy places, which thou hast renewed to us as a new and living way through the veil of the flesh of thy Christ. We therefore, being counted worthy to enter into the place of the tabernacle of thy glory, and to be within the veil and to behold the holy of holies, cast ourselves down before thy goodness.

Chapter Five

The Robe

When Moses went down from Mount Sinai carrying the Ten Commandments, his face was shining because he had been speaking with the Lord; but he did not know it. Aaron and all the people looked at Moses and saw that his face was shining, and they were afraid to go near him. But Moses called to them, and Aaron and all the leaders of the community went to him, and Moses spoke to them. (Ex. 34.29–31)

Moses' face shone when he had been in the presence of the LORD. The account of Moses on Sinai is the earliest record of such an experience, but a similar description of the effect of the LORD's presence occurs in several places. The imagery varies; sometimes it is the face that shines, sometimes it is a robe or garment of light. There can be no doubt that both described the same experience. A few chosen people were able to enter the place of light and the experience transformed them. They became a part of that light. They became heavenly beings.

The most dramatic description of such a transformation is found in *3 Enoch*. There, Rabbi Ishmael sees the angel Metatron in his vision and learns that, before he became an angel, he had been Enoch: 'I am Enoch the son of Jared,' said the great angel, 'and when the generation of the flood sinned and turned to evil deeds and said to God, "Go away. We do not choose to learn your ways," the Holy One, blessed be he, took me from their midst to be a witness against them in the heavenly height... He brought me up in their lifetime, before their very eyes, to the heavenly height, to be a witness against them to future generations.' (*3 Enoch* 4). Enoch/Metatron describes how he was given divine wisdom and understanding and then set to serve before the throne. The Holy One wrapped him in a shining robe and set on his head a crown inscribed with 'the letters which created the world'. This cryptic reference probably means that the crown was inscribed with the four letters of the sacred name. One of the angel's other heavenly names was to be 'the Lesser LORD'. This whole passage seems to be based on the investiture of the high priest. If it is, then what has been suggested about the role of the high priest is correct. In the ritual of the temple he was the LORD, and the ritual par excellence which he performed as the LORD was that of atonement, 'creating' the world.

3 Enoch also describes how Enoch actually became an angel; his material body was burned up by the power of the divine light and he became an incandescent heavenly being.

> When the Holy One, blessed be he, took me to serve the throne of glory, the wheels of the chariot and all the needs of the Shekinah, at once my flesh turned to flame, my sinews to blazing fire, my bones to juniper coals, my eyelashes into lightning flashes, my eyeballs to fiery torches, the hairs of my head to hot flames, all my limbs to wings of burning fire and the substance of my body to a blazing fire. (*3 Enoch* 15)

The earlier Enoch books have a less detailed description of the change; when he saw the light of the throne, Enoch fell on his face, his whole body relaxed and his spirit was transfigured. He cried out and blessed and glorified the Lord. Then he was commissioned to proclaim peace to the earth. He was made a messenger (*1 Enoch* 71).

The Hebrew word for a messenger is also the word for an angel. The tradition of the fiery messenger/angel has ancient roots, but it is only the Enoch literature which makes it clear that human beings sometimes joined their number. The psalmist could have known of it when he wrote: 'Thou makest the winds (spirits) thy messengers, and thy servants flaming fire' (Ps. 104.4). Daniel saw a man clothed in linen whose face was like lightning, his eyes were like flaming torches and his arms and legs had the gleam of burnished bronze (Dan. 10.5–6); he brought Daniel a message 'to make (him) understand what is to befall (his) people in the latter days' (Dan. 10.14). John saw a

man in a long robe with eyes like fire, feet like
burnished bronze and a face like the shining sun;
he gave him a message to take to the seven
churches (Rev. 1.11–16). John recognised the
heavenly messenger as Jesus. It was not only
Enoch who had been taken into the presence of
the throne and transformed; the important detail
in the Enoch tradition is that the transformed
Enoch returned to the world as a heavenly
messenger.

If Jesus had had such a transformation
experience, we should have to look again at the
sayings in the Fourth Gospel which are presently
thought to be the products of later Christian
prophets. Claims to have been in the presence of
God and to act on earth as the Revealer would be
entirely consistent with this tradition (e.g. Jn 3.31–
3). Jesus would then have been conscious of what
he had become: Son of God and Servant. Several
Gospel passages lend themselves to such a
possibility: the account of the baptism suggests
that this was a moment when Jesus became
conscious of Sonship: 'And he was in the
wilderness forty days, tempted by Satan; and he
was with the wild beasts and the angels ministered
unto him' (Mk 1.12–13). These familiar words are
in fact describing an ascent experience; beasts and
ministering angels are exactly what John describes
in his vision of the heavenly throne (Rev 5.6–11).
The account of the forty days alone in the desert
must have come from Jesus himself, presumably
recounted to his disciples at a later date. As a result
of his experience of the creatures of the heavenly
throne and the ministering angels, Jesus too

became the messenger. The Transfiguration was a similar experience, but on that occasion it involved three other disciples (Mk 9.2–8 and parallels).

There is a strange passage in one of the gnostic gospels which may be further evidence that Jesus had experienced this mystical transformation:

> Those who say that the Lord died first and then rose up are in error, for he rose up first and then died. If one does not first attain the resurrection, will he not die? (*The Gospel of Philip* C.G II.3 56)

If Jesus had been 'raised up' to become a heavenly being, like 'Enoch', like the high priestly mystics who contemplated the throne of God, this would explain why there are 'pre-Easter' accounts which resemble post-Easter visions. A small group of disciples would have become fellow mystics, able to describe the experience from within. John was one such; we have his Revelation.

The other transformation image is the robe of light/life. The Great Glory on the throne wore clothes which shone more brightly than the sun and were whiter than any snow (*1 Enoch* 14.20). Psalm 104.1–2 describes the LORD clothed with honour and majesty and covered with light like a garment. Those who stood before the glory reflected its light and had become a part of it; they were also described as men in shining white. Those who left the presence of God lost their robe of glory; thus Adam and Eve, when they left the Garden of Eden were given garments of skin. This did not mean they had clothes made from animal skins, but that they had to have human bodies. By

implication, they had lost their garment of light/
life and thus were cursed with mortality.

On the other hand, when certain people were
granted access to the throne, they were
transformed into heavenly beings and given a
garment of light and eternal life. The transfigured
Jesus was one such: 'His face shone like the sun
and his garments became white as light' (Mt 17.2).
When Enoch was carried into the highest heaven,
he fell and did obeisance before the throne. Then
the LORD sent Michael to him: 'Take Enoch and take
him out of his earthly garments and anoint him
with sweet oil and clothe him in garments of glory.'
He was duly robed and anointed with sweet oil;
'and the appearance of that oil is better than great
light, and its ointment like sweet dew and its smell
like myrrh and shining like the rays of the sun'.
Enoch realised that he had been transformed:

> 'And I looked down,' he said, 'looking at
> myself, and I was as one of the glorious ones
> and there was no difference. And the terror
> and trembling went away from me and the
> LORD with his mouth summoned me and said:
> "Have courage Enoch; fear not to stand before
> my face to eternity."' (*2 Enoch* 22)

The other description of the robing of Enoch is in
3 Enoch; the angel Metatron describes how the
Great Glory gave him a majestic robe set with
luminaries and a glorious cloak 'in which
brightness, brilliance, splendour and lustre of
every kind were fixed' (*3 Enoch* 12).

The *Ascension of Isaiah* describes a similar
experience. As he ascended, Isaiah noticed that the

glory of his face was being transformed as he went from heaven to heaven (*Asc. Is.* 7.25). In the sixth heaven he was told by the angel who accompanied him: 'I say to you Isaiah that no man who has to return into a body of that world [has come up or seen] or understood what you have seen and what you are to see...' (*Asc. Is.* 8.11–12). When he finally reached the seventh heaven a voice said: 'The holy Isaiah is permitted to come up here for his robe is here.' He entered and saw 'a wonderful light and also angels without number. And there I saw all the righteous from the time of Adam onwards... And there I saw Enoch and all who were with him, stripped of their robes of the flesh and I saw them in their robes of above. They were like angels who stand there in great glory' (*Asc. Is.* 9.3, 7–9). There were other garments in heaven waiting for the chosen ones: 'And I saw many robes placed there, and many thrones and many crowns and I said to the angel who led me, "Whose are these robes and thrones and crowns?" And he said to me, "As for these robes, there are many from that world who will receive them through believing in the words of that one who will be named as I have told you"' (*Asc. Is.* 9.24–5).

When Enoch saw the throne visions, he was told of the elect who would rise from the earth; 'And they shall have been clothed with garments of glory, and these shall be the garments of life from the LORD of Spirits' (*1 Enoch* 62.16). The most explicit Christian version of this belief is found in the two chapters added by a Christian writer to a Jewish text of Ezra's visions. (The book exists under various names, but is found in the

Apocrypha as *2 Esdras*). Ezra sees the glorious garments which await the faithful in heaven:

> Rise and stand and see at the feast of the Lord the number of those who have been sealed. Those who have departed from the shadow of this age have received glorious garments from the Lord. Take again your full number, O Zion, and conclude the list of your people who are clothed in white, who have fulfilled the Law of the Lord.' (*2 Esdras* 2.38–40)

A tall young man, identified by the accompanying angel as the Son of God, gives each a crown. 'These,' he says, 'are they who have put off mortal clothing and have put on the immortal and they have confessed the name of God; now they are being crowned and receive palms' (*2 Esdras* 2.45). The unfortunate man in the parable of the king's feast (Mt 22.11–14), who was thrown out because he had no wedding garment, was someone who had tried to have a place in heaven without a robe of light.

Both images of transformation passed easily into early Christian thought. The light, as John said, had come into the world, and so it was no longer just the chosen few who were permitted to behold the glory. The real significance of John's words is sometimes missed; Moses had asked to see the glory and been told that it was not possible: 'While my glory passes by I will put you in a cleft of the rock and I will cover you with my hand until I have passed by' (Ex. 33.22). John, however, was emphatic: 'We *have* beheld his glory, the glory as of the only Son from the Father' (Jn 1.14). He uses different language in his first letter, but, given the equivalents derived from temple imagery, what he says is the same: 'The life was revealed and we saw it and testify to it and proclaim to you the eternal life which was with the Father and was revealed to us...' (1 Jn 1.2). Apart from the 'light is life' symbolism of the temple, this latter statement makes no sense; how can 'life' be revealed? There can be no doubt that the glory seen in Jesus was the 'glory' in the holy of holies. Commenting on Isaiah, John says: 'Isaiah said this because he saw his glory and spoke of him' (Jn 12.41). The only time Isaiah saw the glory was in his temple vision, when he saw the King, the LORD of Hosts (Is. 6).

The implication of this is that the transforming effect of the glory is now available to all; those who have seen the glory have been changed from this life to the life of heaven. They have become angels, or, in the language of the visionaries, they have become sons of God: 'But to all who received him, who believed in his name, he gave power to become children of God' (Jn 1.12). Thus for John, 'seeing the glory' is equivalent to Paul's 'receiving the Spirit' (Rom. 8.14–15). Elsewhere Paul also refers to transformation by the glory: 'The LORD Jesus Christ will change our lowly body to be like his glorious body...' (Phil. 3.21); and 'And we all, with unveiled faces, reflecting the glory of the LORD are being changed into his likeness from one degree of glory to another; for this comes from the LORD who is the Spirit' (2 Cor. 3.17–18).

The new life, or the new nature, was put on like the robe of light. 'This imperishable nature must put on the imperishable and this mortal nature must put on immortality' (1 Cor. 15.53) is one of Paul's descriptions, as he tries to explain to the Corinthian churches what is meant by life after death. Showing how this different life affects behaviour, he writes to the church at Colossae: 'You have put on the new *man*, which is being renewed in knowledge after the image of its creator' (Col. 3.10). Here the reference is to the gift of Wisdom which flows in the river from the throne, the wisdom which makes human beings like God. To the Ephesians he writes: 'Put off your old *man* which belongs to your former manner of life and is corrupt through deceitful lusts, and be renewed in the spirit of your minds, and put on the new *man* created after the likeness of God in true righteousness and holiness' (Eph. 4.22–4). Here the reference is to the experience of Enoch, when Michael was told to take off his earthly garments and robe him with light. The preferred modern translation 'nature' is anaemic in comparison with the literal 'man' at this point and does not convey so well the force of the original imagery. Other variations on the theme are: 'put on Christ' (Rom. 13.14; Gal. 3.27) and 'put on love' (Col. 3.14).

The robes of light are mentioned most frequently in the book of Revelation which, as a vision of the throne, is their natural setting. There is the LORD's promise to those in Sardis who 'have not soiled their garments' that they will walk with him in white (Rev. 3.4). The elders around the throne have white garments and golden crowns (Rev. 4.4). The saints beneath the altar are given a white robe and told to rest until their number is complete. The great multitude before the throne wear white and carry palms (Rev. 7.9). They have washed their robes and made them white with the blood of the Lamb. The blood of the great Day of Atonement, in other words, has given all believers access to the throne and they have their new life. In chapter 14 we learn something more about this multitude; they have the Name of the Lamb and his Father written on their foreheads. In other words, they have the letters of the sacred Name which had formerly been worn by the high priest. Like him, they wear white in the holy place.

The coming of the glory into the world had not only brought light and life to all who saw it; it had also given to all believers the role of the ancient high priests. They were the new 'holy priesthood' (1 Pet. 2.5), the 'royal priesthood... called out of darkness into his marvellous light' (1 Pet. 2.9) 'Since we have confidence to enter the sanctuary by the blood of Jesus, by the new and living way which he opened for us through the curtain, that is, through his flesh' (Heb. 10.19–20). Anyone who lived the life of the holy of holies, eternal life, was an angel, a messenger, a mediator of the new covenant. That is why the Christians called themselves 'children of God' (Jn 1.12; Rom. 8. 14), and 'saints' i.e. 'holy ones' (Rom. 1.7; 1 Cor. 1.2; Eph. 1.1; Phil. 1.1; Col. 1.2).

All this imagery appears in its original setting in the closing words of the New Testament. The Great Atonement has taken place; evil has been judged and the creation renewed. The heavenly temple functions again in all its splendour as the source of light and life:

Then he showed me the river of the water of life, bright as crystal, flowing from the throne of God and of the Lamb through the middle of the street of the city; also on either side of the river the tree of life with its twelve kinds of fruits, yielding its fruit each month; and the leaves of the tree were for the healing of the nations. There shall no more be anything accursed, but the throne of God and of the Lamb shall be in it and his servants shall worship him; they shall see his face and his name shall be on their foreheads. And night shall be no more; they need no light of lamp or sun for the LORD God will be their light and they shall reign for ever and ever. (Rev. 22.1–5)

Postscript

The relationship between the Old Testament and the New has yet to be explained. Although Marcion's efforts to remove the Old Testament from the church in the second century were unsuccessful, he cast a long shadow; his attitude to the Old Testament is still a powerful but unacknowledged influence on New Testament scholars. It has, for example, become fashionable in some circles to see the 'Christ cult' and its New Testament as the product of a non-Palestinian post-Jewish society somewhere in the Mediterranean world. The original Jesus people may even have been the followers of a wandering cynic philosopher in Galilee and so on. This does not add up. If the churches chose to keep the Old Testament (and it was a conscious choice, not something they kept because nobody got around to throwing it out), there must have been a reason for it. Further, the Jewish communities in the second century made new Greek translations of the Old Testament and it is widely supposed that this was done because Christians used the existing Greek version. There were accusations on both sides that texts had been altered, suggesting that the fundamentals of Christianity were being demonstrated from the Old Testament even in a non-Palestinian, post-Jewish society.

As currently described and studied, however, there is no organic link between the two which would have made the Old Testament either fundamental or even useful to the early church. What is taught as 'Old Testament' today has little or no bearing on the New Testament and Christian origins. As a result, there are those who think that the New Testament can be taught and even understood without any knowledge of the Old. The results are plain for all to see.

Old Testament study is, and must be, an autonomous discipline; nevertheless, a major aspect, namely how it gave rise to the New Testament, is neglected. Since the majority of Old Testament users worldwide are Christian faith communities, much of what is done in the field of Old Testament study is perceived as irrelevant to them. In a consumer-led society, this has to be an unwise course to pursue.

The most obvious link between the Old Testament and the New is the Christian claim that the Old Testament, in particular its prophecies, had been fulfilled. Luke's Jesus explains from the Old Testament how the Messiah had to suffer to enter his glory (Lk 24.26–7). What texts did he use? The conventional account of how the Old Testament was understood in first-century Palestine does not include a suffering Messiah. And what of the atonement? Did this fundamental belief originate in the Palestinian community or did it develop from contacts with pagan redeemer cults? The most obvious source for both would have been a temple-based system; the Messiah was the royal figure of the older cult and atonement was the greatest ritual of the temple year, and yet concrete proof of both is lacking.

The shape of Christian theology had been established in the first generation which suggests that the fundamentals were available to the Palestinian community in the ways they had seen their scriptures fulfilled. There are two possible descriptions of their use of scripture; either they made a novel selection of texts and themes from which they argued for their new beliefs; or they knew of an existing set of texts and themes which we no longer recognise but which they saw fulfilled in Jesus and proclaimed as their new faith. The latter seems more likely as it is consistent with another phenomenon.

There are elements in the writings of the first two Christian centuries which are not in the New Testament and yet were claimed as the authentic tradition. Ignatius of Antioch, for example, writing to the Trallians early in the second century, claimed knowledge of 'celestial secrets, angelic hierarchies and the dispositions of the heavenly powers' (*Trallians* 5). At the end of the second century Irenaeus, that champion of orthodoxy and scourge of gnosticism included in his account of the true faith a description of the seven heavens, their powers, angels and archangels (*Proof of the Apostolic Preaching* 9). Their similarity to angel texts now known from Palestine and Egypt indicates that this teaching could have been part of the original Christianity, another way of understanding the Old Testament. A period of oral transmission for the material in the Gospels is accepted almost without question; can we assume, also without question, that everything in that oral tradition was written down? I think not. So often it is assumed that the New Testament gives a comprehensive picture of early belief, forgetting that much of Paul's writing was to clarify obscurities or justify his innovations. The greater part of the teaching, accepted without dispute, could have remained oral and thus the real nature of Palestinian Christianity is a great unknown, except where it breaks the surface in fixed formulae and fragments of what may have been hymns. In addition, there was a 'secret tradition' known to Clement of Alexandria and Origen; it has remained a secret, but the very fact that there was such a tradition is a stark reminder that we do not know everything. The book of Revelation is another unknown; how did such a complex piece of temple-based apocalyptic material come to be accepted in the churches as a revelation from Jesus himself? The common factor in all these unknowns is the temple tradition.

Then there is the question of the Dead Sea Scrolls and the picture they give of first-century Palestine. Until their recovery, the society from which Christianity emerged had been reconstructed using early rabbinic texts even though they had been written many generations later. This produced a doubly distorted picture: it was a massive anachronism and it was only one part of the picture, there being no extant writings from the Sadducees or any other priestly group. As the Qumran materials have become available, so it has become clear that first-century Judaism was not at all like the received picture. The issue at Qumran was the temple; the ideology was apocalyptic and the poetry and hymns were inspired by the temple vision of heaven and earth.

There has also been the revival of interest in apocalyptic and other non-canonical texts, especially when fragments from Qumran confirmed that some of these were pre-Christian. These texts had been edited, augmented and preserved only by the Christians, even though not originally written by them. They must have been part of the pre-Christian tradition in Palestine which was important for the early church but abandoned by Judaism. It was also suggested, on other grounds, that apocalyptic had been the mother of all Christian theology, that the writings which had been virtually marginalised by serious scholars and main-line churches were in fact central to understanding Christian origins. Apocalyptic writings originated in the temple cult.

These three factors, which in reality are three aspects of one question, necessitate a massive reappraisal of Christian origins. We must focus on the first-generation Palestinian community, absorbing the implications of the theology emerging from Qumran and the non-canonical texts. What emerges is the possibility that it was temple theology (rather than 'apocalyptic', which is only one aspect of it) which gave rise to Christianity.

Many of the books compiled during or after the exile had been hostile to the old temple and

monarchy and these books formed the bulk of the
canon when it was eventually defined. Material
which was excluded from the canon has often been
dismissed by scholars as foreign, sectarian or a late
and degenerate addition to the pure tradition of
Israel. Even though it was known that the canon
was not defined until a relatively late date, the
notion of 'canon' has been retrojected onto the
Second Temple period and what later became
'canonical' has become the unacknowledged
measure by which the earlier period is defined.
Much of this excluded material can now be
recognised as a relic of the older temple and royal
cult, not in the sense that it is a direct survival from
the period of the first temple, but rather that it is
an expression of temple theology and proof of a
living and growing tradition in the period of the
second temple. Who wrote this material and where
is another question.

   Yet other questions are: what happened to the
theology of the second temple? Assuming that
their contribution to the Pentateuch and
Chronicles was written at the beginning of the
Second Temple period, did the priesthood in
Jerusalem produce nothing for four centuries? And
if they did, where is it? Why was it not eventually
included in the canon? Why, indeed, was so much
'temple' material specifically excluded? Is it
coincidence that Christians based their theology
on the older cult of sacrifice, described Jesus as
the great high priest, developed their own concept
of priesthood and kept the books which Judaism
chose to exclude? These questions are not asked
because Protestant Christianity in particular has

felt more at home with the religion of the Law than with the religion of the priests, their rituals and visions. The Old Testament, as later defined, felt comfortable and the difficult gap between the Old Testament and Christianity was bridged with considerable ingenuity. The questions about the real relationship of Old Testament and New are uncomfortable, but they must be asked.

A study of the translations of Proverbs 29.18 illustrates well the problem both in its ancient and its modern form. The Authorised Version has: 'Where there is no vision the people perish.' The Revised Standard Version has: 'Where there is no prophecy the people cast off restraint.' The New English Bible has: 'Where there is no one in authority, the people break loose.' The Today's English Version has: 'A nation without guidance is a nation without order.' The Hebrew original is literally: 'In the absence of a vision/visionary the people is let loose' and yet none of the recent versions chooses to use the word 'vision'. The RSV has 'prophecy' which has some justification in that there is an explanatory note in 1 Samuel 9.9 'He who is now called a prophet was formerly called a seer.' Whenever this was written, the people did not know what was meant by a seer. By the fourth century the prophets were ashamed to admit that they had had visions (Zech. 13.4), even though the visionary texts of *1 Enoch* probably originated at this time. When the Greek version of Proverbs was made, the word chosen for 'seer' was 'interpreter of oracles', 'exegete' which now means an interpreter of the written scriptures. The NEB chooses 'one in authority' which does not convey the idea of vision at all and the TEV's 'God's guidance' is adequate but colourless.

Thus the vision, and with it the temple tradition, has disappeared from the Bible in more senses than one. After the exile the nature of prophecy changed; the prophets were no longer people of vision but a body of writings to be interpreted according to set rules. The nature of their authority changed as the written word replaced the image and theology became a matter of words and even letters. Finer and finer points were discussed and the vision was confined to the 'outside books' where it has remained ever since. This is one strand of Israel's religion, the one which accounts for the present contents of the Old Testament.

There must have been another to account for the non-canonical books and theology (theologies?) emerging from the Qumran material. This must have been the temple tradition, strange because temple theology is largely unknown as such, but sufficiently familiar to excite curiosity. *What is recognisable in temple theology is what we know as Christianity.* Having established a considerable degree of correspondence between the two, we may eventually be able to use primitive Christian texts to reconstruct the earlier traditions of Judaism.

Index